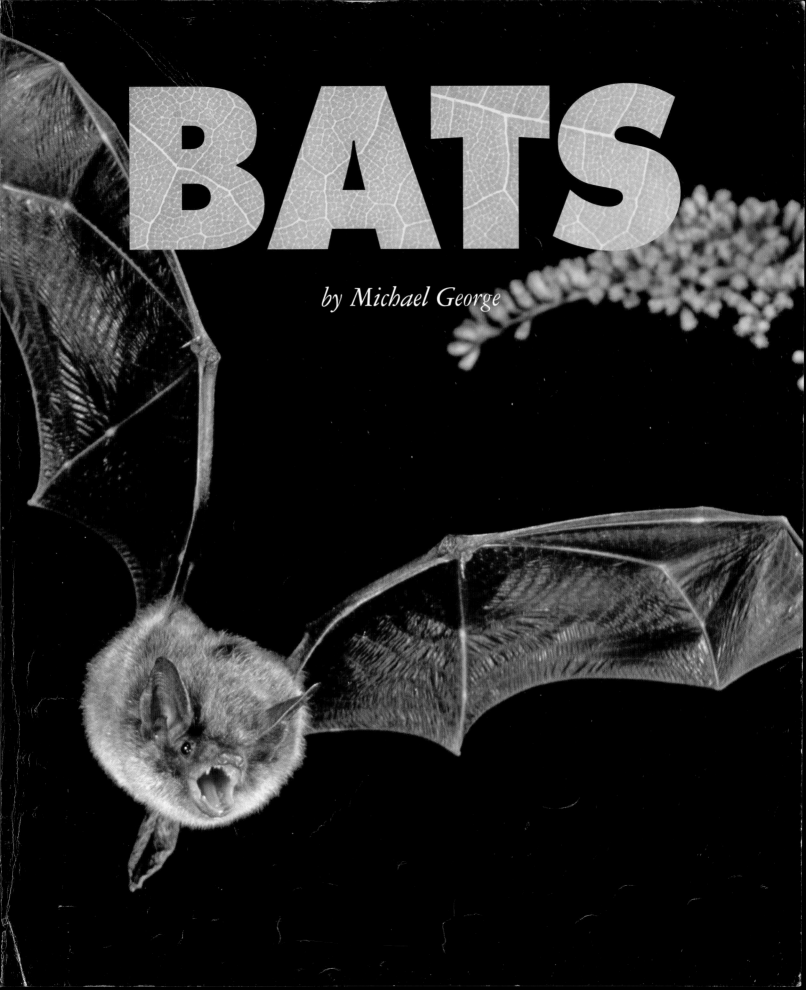

BATS

by Michael George

The Child's World

Content Adviser:
Dick Mills,
World Discovery Safaris

Published in the United States of America by The Child's World®
PO Box 326 • Chanhassen, MN 55317-0326
800-599-READ • www.childsworld.com

PHOTO CREDITS
© Arco Images/Alamy: 9
© Bryan Knox; Papilio/Corbis: 13
© David A. Northcott/Corbis: 21
© Dr. Merlin D. Tuttle/Bat Conservation International/
        Photo Researchers, Inc.: 14–15, 18
© Dr. Merlin D. Tuttle/Photo Researchers, Inc.: 16, 19
© Gerard Lacz/Peter Arnold, Inc./Alamy: 23
© Jack Jeffrey/Photo Resource Hawaii/Alamy: 27
© Joe McDonald/Corbis: cover, 1, 4–5, 10–11
© John R. MacGregor/Peter Arnold, Inc./Alamy: 24–25
© Michael & Patricia Fogden/Corbis: 17
© Robert and Linda Mitchell: 28
© Theo Allofs/Corbis: 7

ACKNOWLEDGMENTS
The Child's World®: Mary Berendes, Publishing Director;
Katherine Stevenson, Editor

The Design Lab: Kathleen Petelinsek, Design and Page Production

LIBRARY OF CONGRESS CATALOGING-IN-PUBLICATION DATA
George, Michael, 1964–
 Bats / by Michael George.
    p. cm. — (New naturebooks)
 Includes bibliographical references and index.
 ISBN 1-59296-631-4 (library bound : alk. paper)
 1. Bats—Juvenile literature. I. Title. II. Series.
 QL737.C5G2963 2006
 599.4—dc22   2006001359

Table of Contents

On the cover: Little brown bats like this one are common in the United States and Canada.

Meet the Bat!

Bats have been around for about 50 million years.

It's a warm, summer evening, and you're sitting on your porch watching the sun go down. A mosquito buzzes by your head, and then another. You swat them away, but more seem to keep coming. Suddenly, something larger flies by. The animal looks like a bird—but not quite. As you watch, it darts around, flying first one way and then another. It is eating the mosquitoes! What is this flying creature? It's a bat!

This little brown bat is hunting flying insects at night in Pennsylvania. These small bats are only about 3 inches (8 cm) long.

What Are Bats?

Bats flap their wings by using muscles on their backs. Birds use the muscles on their chests instead.

The scientific name for bats, *Chiroptera* (ki-ROP-ter-uh), means "hand wing."

Bats belong to a group of animals called **mammals**. Mammals have warm bodies and feed their babies milk from their bodies. Most mammals have hair or fur all over their bodies. People, cats, and dogs are mammals, too.

Bats are different from other mammals, however—they are the only mammals with wings! These wings are made of thin, tough skin. If you look carefully, a bat's wings look a lot like your hands. The four bones inside the wings are actually long finger bones. Bats also have a thumb. This thumb has a sharp, hooked toenail which the bat uses for climbing and for grooming itself.

Here you can see a bat called a grey-headed flying fox. Put your right hand on top of its wing and line up your fingers with the bat's long, skinny bones. Can you see how its wing is much like your hand?

Are There Different Kinds of Bats?

The smallest mammal in the world is the bumblebee bat. It lives in Thailand and weighs just .07 ounces (2 grams). That's lighter than a penny!

Mexican free-tailed bats can fly as high as 10,000 feet (3,048 m).

There are nearly a thousand different kinds, or **species**, of bats! Bats come in many different shapes and sizes. Some are smaller than your hand. Others have a huge **wingspan**. A bat's wingspan is the distance from one wing tip to the other. Some bats have wingspans nearly six feet (2 m) across!

Many bats are brown or black, but a few are colorful shades of orange or red. Some bats have cute fuzzy faces and little feet. Others have long ears and strange-looking noses.

8

Grey-headed flying foxes like this one are just one of several different types of flying foxes. Named for their foxlike snouts, flying foxes weigh about two pounds (1 kg) and have wingspans of almost six feet (2 m). Flying foxes live in the warm jungles of southeast Asia and northern Australia.

Where Do Bats Live?

Honduran white bats create "tents" out of leaves. These shelters protect the bats from the heavy jungle rains. The bats might live in their "tents" for several weeks before moving to another area.

Bats live in almost every country of the world. The only places without bats are cold, treeless polar areas and a few islands in the ocean. Bats like warm areas where there are lots of places to hide and plenty of food for them to eat.

Although bats live nearly everywhere, few people ever see them. That's because bats are **nocturnal** animals—they sleep during the day and are active at night. Most bats **roost**, or rest, in dark, out-of-the-way places. They especially like to roost in hollow trees, caves, attics, barns, and even under bridges. At night, they leave their roosts and fly out in search of food.

These little brown bats are roosting in the ceiling of a church in Pennsylvania.

How Do Bats Sleep?

In areas with cold winters, bats go into a long, deep sleep called hibernation. Their heartbeat and breathing slow down, and they can live for three to four months without eating. They wake up when the weather gets warmer and they can once more find food.

Bats sleep hanging upside down. Sharp claws on their back feet let them cling to beams, branches, or even cave ceilings. A few types of bats like to sleep alone. But many bats roost in large groups called **colonies**. Some colonies contain more than 10 million bats!

Bats wake up just as the sun is setting. They squeak and chatter as they clean their fur. Bats groom themselves like cats, licking their fur and wings to help them stay soft and clean. When the sun finally sets, the bats leave their hiding places and fly out into the night.

These common fruit bats are roosting in a cave in Thailand. You can see how they are using their back feet to cling to the bumpy cave wall.

What Do Bats Eat?

Flying foxes are fruit-eating bats. These large bats require lots of food. They must often fly great distances to find enough to eat—sometimes over 30 miles (48 km) a night! Many flying foxes smell like rotten fruit, an odor that helps keep enemies away.

Different kinds of bats eat different kinds of food. Some bats that live in warmer areas eat only fruit. Some fruit-eating bats grow to be very large.

Other bats eat **nectar**, a sweet liquid found in flowers. Most nectar-eating bats are small. They have pointed noses and long tongues that help them reach deep into flowers. Nectar-eating bats often get powdery **pollen** on their faces. As the bats go from flower to flower, they spread the pollen and pick up more. Spreading pollen helps the plants make seeds.

Here you can see a lesser long-nosed bat eating a cactus fruit. These rare bats live in the deserts of the southern United States and Central America.

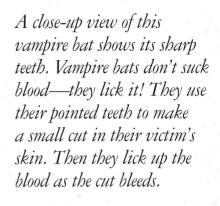

A close-up view of this vampire bat shows its sharp teeth. Vampire bats don't suck blood—they lick it! They use their pointed teeth to make a small cut in their victim's skin. Then they lick up the blood as the cut bleeds.

Not all bats eat plant foods. Some live off animal foods instead. Some large bats in the jungle eat small animals such as mice, frogs, lizards, and birds. Other bats eat fish. They swoop over water and hook fish with their sharp claws. A few bats that live in Central and South America even feed on blood! These vampire bats make small bites in the skin of animals such as horses or cows, then lick up the drops of blood.

Many bats, including most of those in North America, eat flies, mosquitoes, and other annoying insects. They also eat moths and beetles that can destroy farmers' crops. A single bat can eat more than 600 bugs in one hour!

Some kinds of frogs are highly poisonous, so frog-eating bats must be very careful about which frogs they eat! The bats can tell the difference between safe and poisonous frogs by listening to the male frogs' calls.

This Niceforo's big-eared bat has caught a grasshopper to eat. These bats live in Central and South America.

17

How Do Bats Fly in the Dark?

Tiger moths make clicks that sound like the noises bats make. The clicks seem to confuse bats that might want to eat the moths.

To catch tiny insects, bats must be expert flyers. They can dive through tight spaces without bumping into anything—even in the dark! How do they do that? By using **echolocation**.

As they fly, bats send out very high squeaks through their mouths or noses. The squeaks are too high-pitched for us to hear. These sounds bounce off objects and return to the bat as echoes. By listening to these echoes, bats can find objects on the ground and in the air. They can find food even on the darkest nights.

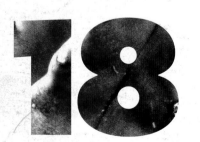

This page: California leaf-nosed bats have huge ears! These bats live in the southern U.S. and northern Mexico.

Opposite page: This California leaf-nosed bat has used echolocation to find a bug to eat.

What Are Baby Bats Like?

Mother bats can't fly well with their heavy babies clinging to them. When it's time to hunt, all of the colony's mother bats leave their babies behind in the roost. When the mothers return, each one must find her baby—which looks exactly like thousands of other babies! Each mother finds her own baby by its smell and its cry.

In many bat colonies, all of the females give birth to their babies at the same time. Mother bats usually have one baby at a time, but sometimes they have twins. Right after it's born, a baby bat crawls up its mother's belly and clings to her fur. For the next few weeks, this is where the baby lives. The baby drinks its mother's milk and sleeps right on her belly.

Baby bats grow quickly. Some young bats are able to fly and feed themselves after just 18 days. Other young bats stay with their mothers for up to nine months. When a young bat is ready, it begins to fly and to feed itself. It stays in the same colony as its mother and other relatives.

20

Here you can see a baby Egyptian fruit bat as it clings to its mother's belly. Egyptian fruit bats live in huge colonies made up of thousands of bats.

Are Bats Dangerous?

Since bats fly at night and live in dark or hidden places, people have always thought they were scary. Instead of learning more about bats, people began to make up stories about them. That's one reason why bats appear in scary movies and spooky decorations on Halloween.

For hundreds of years, people thought bats were dangerous animals. They believed bats got tangled in people's hair or were spooky creatures that attacked people in the night. The truth is, bats are shy animals that prefer to be left alone. Swooping bats aren't attacking people—they're hunting and chasing insects. And bats are excellent flyers—they would never land in your hair by mistake.

22

Greater mouse-eared bats like these are common in Europe. Here you can see two bats hunting for insects on a dark night.

Like other wild animals, bats sometimes carry diseases that can make people very sick. *Rabies* is a serious disease carried by a small number of bats—less than one out of every 200. Other animals such as skunks, raccoons, dogs, and cats sometimes carry rabies, too. Animals with rabies can pass the disease to people by biting them. In the United States, about one person a year dies from a rabid bat bite. The body waste of some bats, called *guano* (GWAH-noh), can also make people sick.

To stay on the safe side, never touch or hold a wild bat. If you see a sick bat, leave it alone. You might hurt the bat even more if you try to pick it up or help it.

If a bat gets into your house, what should you do? If the bat is trying to escape, try turning off the lights and opening some doors and windows so it can find its way out. If that doesn't work, most communities have animal control officers that can help or tell you what to do.

Big brown bats like this one are common throughout North and Central America. These insect-eaters have very sharp teeth and they could give you a painful bite if you got too close!

25

Are Bats in Danger?

Sometimes special gates are put across the entrances to caves where bats are known to roost. The gates keep people out, but bats can fly in and out easily.

Worldwide, bat numbers are shrinking. Many bat species are **endangered**, which means there are few of them left in the wild. As more people move into areas where bats live, the bats lose their roosting and hibernating places. Sometimes bats find new places to roost, such as under bridges or inside attics. But bats that try to make new homes in houses or buildings are often seen as pests—and are often killed.

Many countries now have programs to protect bats. Areas have been set aside for bats to roost and raise their young in safety. With time, it's hoped that bats of all kinds will make a comeback!

Here you can see an endangered Hawaiian hoary bat as it roosts in a tree. These insect-eating bats have been listed as endangered since 1970, and their numbers are still very low.

Because there are so many scary ideas about bats, many people are afraid of them. The truth is, bats aren't mean or evil creatures. If you're lucky enough to see a bat, don't scream or run for cover. Instead, watch the bat as it swoops and flies. Then let the bat go on its way. It might eat some of the mosquitoes that would otherwise bite you!

The common little brown bat can live for more than 20 years.

Bats were once called "flittermice." That's because people thought of them as flying mice.

Here you can see Mexican free-tailed bats as they leave their cave for the night. These bats are common in the southern United States, Mexico, and Central and South America.

Glossary

colonies (KOLL-uh-neez) Colonies are large groups of animals. Some bat colonies contain thousands or even millions of bats.

echolocation (ek-oh-loh-KAY-shun) Echolocation is the process of locating something by sending out sounds and listening for the echoes that come back. Bats use echolocation to hunt and fly at night.

endangered (en-DAYN-jurd) When a kind of animal is endangered, it is in danger of dying out. Many bat species are endangered.

hibernation (hy-bur-NAY-shun) Hibernation is a long, deep sleep some animals experience during winter months. Bats in colder areas hibernate.

mammals (MAM-mulz) Mammals are animals that have warm bodies and feed their babies milk from their bodies. Bats, dogs, cats, and people are all mammals.

nectar (NEK-ter) Nectar is a sweet liquid found in flowers. Some bats like to eat nectar.

nocturnal (nok-TURN-ull) Nocturnal animals are active at night rather than in the day. Bats and owls are nocturnal.

pollen (POL-len) Pollen is a yellow powder that flowers produce as part of their process for making seeds. Nectar-eating bats carry pollen from plant to plant as they feed.

roost (ROOST) When an animal roosts, it rests. Bats like to roost in dark, damp places.

species (SPEE-sheez) A species is a different kind of a certain animal. There are almost a thousand different species of bats.

wingspan (WING-span) An animal's wingspan is the distance from one wing tip to the other. Some bats have huge wingspans.

To Find Out More

Read It!

Gibbons, Gail. *Bats.* New York: Holiday House, 1999.

Maestro, Betsy, and Giulio Maestro (illustrator). *Bats: Night Fliers.* New York: Scholastic, 1994.

McNulty, Faith, and Lena Shiffman (illustrator). *When I Lived with Bats.* New York: Scholastic, 1998.

Milton, Joyce, and Judith Moffatt (illustrator). *Bats: Creatures of the Night.* New York: Grosset & Dunlap, 1993.

Selsam, Millicent Ellis, and Joyce Hunt. *A First Look at Bats.* New York: Walker, 1991.

On the Web

Visit our home page for lots of links about bats:
http://www.childsworld.com/links

Note to Parents, Teachers, and Librarians: We routinely check our Web links to make sure they're safe, active sites—so encourage your readers to check them out!

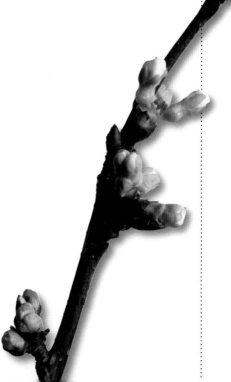

31

Index